◆

"From the age of six I had a mania
for drawing the shapes of things.
When I was fifty I had published a universe of designs,
but all I have done before the age of seventy
is not worth bothering with.
At seventy-five I'll have learned something
of the pattern of nature, of animals, of plants,
of trees, birds, fish, and insects.
When I am eighty you will see real progress.
At ninety I shall have cut my way
deeply into the mystery of life itself.
At a hundred I shall be a marvelous artist.
At a hundred and ten everything I create—a dot,
a line—will jump to life as never before."

—Katsushika Hokusai

SHAHZIA SIKANDER. *The Scroll.*
1991–92. Vegetable color, dry pigment, watercolor, and tea on hand-prepared "wasli" paper. 16⅛" × 63⅞".
Courtesy of Sikkema Jenkins & Co.

COME LOOK WITH ME

Asian Art

Kimberly Lane

iᴎi Charlesbridge

For Harris
—K. L.

Published by Charlesbridge
85 Main Street
Watertown, MA 02472
(617) 926-0329
www.charlesbridge.com

Library of Congress Cataloging-in-Publication Data
Lane, Kimberly.
     Come look with me : Asian art / Kimberly Lane.
         p. cm.
     ISBN 978-1-890674-19-9 (reinforced for library use)
     1. Art, Asian—Juvenile literature. 2. Art appreciation—
Juvenile literature. I. Title.
N7260.L27 2008
709.5—dc22   2007037926

Printed in China
(hc) 10 9 8 7 6 5 4 3 2 1

Production & Design: Charles Davey *design* LLC

Contents

Preface

To delve into the history of art in Asia is to travel across thousands of years in time and through the rich traditions of many cultures. This book presents a selection of Asian artworks, focusing on the arts of countries in South, East, and Southeast Asia. Travelers and merchants crisscrossed Asia on well-worn routes such as the Silk Road, and along with their wares, they carried a variety of artistic traditions. An idea or technique that began in one culture was often adapted or altered by cultures in other regions and subsequent generations.

Throughout history the arts of Asia have had a wide variety of purposes, including religious use, functional utility, education, and aesthetic enjoyment. Figures and themes of major religions such as Buddhism, Hinduism, and Islam feature prominently as the subjects of works of art. Societal codes and values are reflected in artworks created by the artists who lived in a particular place at a particular time. To promote better understanding, the cultural and religious contexts for the artworks as well as biographical information about the artists have been provided whenever possible.

The artworks selected for this book are examples that will speak to children. Some are many hundreds of years old, while others were created by artists working today. It is not meant to be comprehensive or even representative of the vast diversity of art from all of Asia, but to be a compelling introduction to the rich artistic traditions of this part of the world, and to provide children with the opportunity to venture into new ways of thinking about art and the world around them.

How to use this book

COME LOOK WITH ME: *Asian Art* is part of a series of art appreciation books for children. This book presents an interactive way of looking at art. Each of the twelve artists is represented by a full-page color plate, which is accompanied by a brief biography and information about the artwork. The titles of the art reproduced in this book appear exactly as they are used by the institutions or individuals who own the original artworks. The text may be read aloud by an adult or paraphrased to help guide children's conversations.

In addition to the background information, each image is paired with a set of questions intended to encourage thoughtful observation and to stimulate conversation between adults and children. Like others in this series, this book may be shared with one child or a group of children. Ask a child to point to specific parts of an image while they discuss it. If working with a group, ask the children to share their ideas. There are no right or wrong answers to the questions, and everyone will benefit from the different perspectives. To keep the interaction lively, it is best to limit each session to the discussion of two or three artworks.

This book can be used at home, in the classroom, or in museums. Whenever possible, it is ideal to see an artwork in person. The methods given here provide children with a way of looking at original works of art and encourage them to share their understanding with others.

After XIE HUAN (ca. 1370–ca. 1450). *Elegant Gathering in the Apricot Garden.* [Detail.]
ca. 1437, Ming dynasty (1368–1644). Handscroll; ink and color on silk.
14⁹⁄₁₆" × 95¾". Overall with mounting: 14¾" × 503¼".
The Metropolitan Museum of Art, Purchase, The Dillon Fund Gift, 1989 (1989.141.3).
Photograph © 1995 The Metropolitan Museum of Art.

8

How many people do you see in this scene? What are they all doing?

Who do you think might be the most important people?

Where is this scene taking place?

Why are some parts of the painting in color while others are not?

On April 6, 1437, Yang Rong, a powerful court official, hosted a gathering for eight of his colleagues in the famous garden of his home in the city of Beijing. Yang Rong and the other important officials and ministers served the emperor of China, the supreme leader of the Chinese empire. At this gathering, Yang Rong invited his guests to participate in respected activities of educated men, such as viewing paintings and calligraphy (artistic writing), writing poetry, and playing chess.

We know of the events of this day because they are recorded in this handscroll painting, *Elegant Gathering in the Apricot Garden*, by the artist Xie Huan. A handscroll is a roll of paper or silk that is viewed by unrolling it one section at a time, moving from right to left horizontally. For this handscroll, the artist used a brush to apply ink and colored pigments to silk to create the image. This handscroll also includes colophons (comments or poems) by each of the participants written in honor of this festive day. Copies of the painting would have been made for all of the guests at the gathering, and the painting shown here may have been one of those copies.

In this image we see one portion of the long handscroll. In the center are three men. Their ceremonial robes of red, blue, and black, and their black hats, called *wusha mao*, indicate that they are important officials. In fact these three are Yang Rong and two of his guests. To the right of the three officials three servants stand near a table set with a small landscape painting and brushes and ink. Nearby stands a black-necked crane, an ancient Chinese symbol of long life and good fortune. Around the figures are a variety of rocks and plants from the garden. Garden design was considered an art practiced by the wealthy and well-educated, and a beautiful garden enhanced the status of its owner.

秋菊有佳色裛露掇其英況此忘憂物
遠我遺世情一觴雖獨進杯盡壺自傾
日入群動息歸鳥趨林鳴嘯傲東軒下
聊復得此生
新羅山人子錄陶句

The translation of the poem reads:

The fall chrysanthemums have lovely colors.
I pluck the petals that are wet with dew,
And float them in this Care Dispelling Thing
To strengthen my resolve to leave the world.
I drink my solitary cup alone
And when it's empty, pour myself another.
The sun goes down, and all of nature rests.
Homing birds fly chirping toward the grove.
I sit complacent on the east veranda,
Having somehow found my life again.

HUA YEN. *The Red Bird.*
Hanging scroll; ink and color on paper.
49¹⁵⁄₁₆" × 23⁷⁄₁₆".
Princeton University Art Museum.
Gift of Mrs. Edward L. Elliott.
Photograph © 2000
Trustees of Princeton University.
Photo credit: Bruce M. White.

This image is an example of three art forms. What are they?

Where does your eye go first when you look at this painting?

Why do you think the artist used so few colors?

Does reading the poem (a translation of the text in the painting) change the way that you think about this painting?

For thousands of years artworks such as this hanging scroll by Hua Yen (1682–1756) have been prized because they combine three art forms, the "Three Perfections" of painting, poetry, and calligraphy. It was thought that the Three Perfections could express ideas or aspects of a subject better than any of the three could when used alone. Sometimes a painter might choose to illustrate an existing poem, or a poet might be inspired to write a poem about a painting. The poet and painter might be two different people, or they might be the same person. Hua Yen was the son of a paper maker and was born in a small village. He lived most of his life in poverty, traveling extensively and barely making a living from his painting.

The Red Bird is an example of "bird and flower" painting that first became popular in China during the Song dynasty (AD 960–1270). It takes great skill to capture the essence of the subject. The artist uses a soft brush made from animal hairs attached to a bamboo handle to apply black ink to paper or silk. The brush is held vertically, which allows the artist to control the thickness of the brushstrokes by using lighter or heavier pressure. By adding more or less water to the ink, the artist can create a variety of tones from light to dark. Once the ink is applied to the surface it cannot be altered. One false brushstroke could ruin an entire art work.

The same techniques for handling a brush and ink are used in writing calligraphy. This art is greatly admired and has traditionally been considered a purer form of expression than painting.

In the painting on this scroll, a scarlet bird with a sweeping tail is perched among bamboo shoots and chrysanthemum flowers in various tones of black and gray. A poem by Tao Quian in black characters is positioned in the upper left portion of the scroll to balance the painted image.

HUANG MIAOZI. *Untitled.*
1992. Calligraphy of archaic pictograms with the phrase, "The rain-filled clouds cover half the mountain." 25⅕" × 12¼".
Gift of Yang Xianyi. ©1992 The Trustees of The British Museum.

What do some of the symbols in this painting remind you of?

What do you notice in the background?

If you imagine these symbols as a visual language, what do you think they might say?

Unlike languages such as English, Chinese does not have an alphabet of letters. Instead thousands of characters representing different ideas or sounds are combined to create words. Chinese writing is over four thousand years old. The ancient origins of written Chinese characters can be found in pictographs, pictures that represent words or ideas, carved on animal bones and tortoise shells dating from 1550–1000 BC. All the characters can be created by combining eight basic brush strokes in different ways.

In the third and fourth centuries, calligraphy began to be considered an art form in China. The rhythm, line, and structure of each character communicate not only the meaning of a word, but also express the state of mind and feelings of the calligrapher. It can take a lifetime to master the art of calligraphic brushwork.

Huang Miaozi (b. 1913) belongs to a group of calligraphic artists called Modernists, who decided to break free from the strict rules regarding how calligraphic characters should be written. The Modernists began to approach calligraphy more like painting. For example, instead of using only black ink, they included a variety of colored inks, and combined water with their inks to create different effects. They also began to alter the shapes of the characters that they used to make them more interesting artistically.

In this painting Huang first coated his paper with a wash (a thin layer of watery color) of soft colors that creates a feeling of a rainy landscape. Across this surface he has painted the phrase, "The rain-filled clouds cover half the mountain." The characters that he uses are his own versions of ancient pictographs, some of which look a lot like the objects they represent. The viewer can identify the characters for mountain (top left) and rain (bottom right). The small red characters on the left and right are artist's seals. Seals are names, designs, or symbols used to indicate the work's creator or owner.

Bodhisattva, Akashagarbha.
1800–1899. Eastern Tibet. Buddhist Lineage.
Ground mineral pigment on cotton.
19" × 17¼".
Overall with brocade 56" × 27".
© Collection of Rubin Museum of Art.
Photograph © Bruce M. White.

If this painting were telling a story, what do you think happened right before this point? What do you think is about to happen?

Why do you think the large figure in the center is blue?

Where are the different figures looking? How do you think they feel about what they are seeing?

This is an example of a *thangka* from Tibet. The term *thangka* comes from the Tibetan words *than*, meaning "flat," and *ka*, which means "painting." A *thangka* is a flat painting on cloth. The paints used are created by mixing pigments made from crushed minerals and stones with water and animal-skin glue. *Thangkas* are framed in soft silk fabric that allows them to be rolled up like a scroll. The tradition of painting on scrolls developed because of the nomadic lifestyle of the Himalayan peoples. *Thangkas* are easy to pack, unpack, and hang in a new place. We do not know who created this *thangka* because it is unsigned. In Buddhist tradition putting one's signature on a work of art would be considered a sign of ego and pride.

In this *thangka* we see the beautiful bodhisattva, Akashagarbha. In Buddhist teaching a bodhisattva is a spiritual being who has chosen not to reach nirvana, a state of perfect peace. Instead the bodhisattva remains on Earth to help guide others toward enlightenment. Akashagarbha's name means "Essence of Space," and he is one of the eight Great Bodhisattvas.

Akashagarbha sits comfortably on a cushioned wooden throne that appears to be floating above the ground in this peaceful garden. His bright blue skin symbolizes the vast openness of the sky. Around his head shines a large halo, which tells us that he is an important spiritual being. He is clothed in rich robes and adorned with jewels and an intricate golden crown. Near his halo is a smaller figure in green, red, and orange who appears to be flying through the air. In Buddhism it is believed that some very holy people can achieve the ability to fly. We can tell by his orange robe that this flying man is a monk, a member of a religious community. Though Akashagarbha does not seem to notice the monk, the two figures standing on the ground look up at him in astonishment. Scattered on the ground at the bottom of the painting are jewels and other offerings for Akashagarbha.

Seated Ganesha.
14th–15th century. India, Orissa. Ivory. 7¼" × 4¾".
The Metropolitan Museum of Art, Gift of Mr. and Mrs. J. J. Klejman, 1964 (64.102).
Image © The Metropolitan Museum of Art.

Why is there an elephant's head on the body of a person?

What is this figure holding in each of its four hands?

What do you think this sculpture might be made of?

This statue is a holy image of Ganesha, a powerful and popular Hindu god. Hinduism is a religion that began in India thousands of years ago. There are many different Hindu gods who each have special powers and abilities to help humans. Ganesha is the god of good luck and wisdom, and is known for his ability to solve problems. People often leave offerings and pray to him to help them when they begin something new.

There are many different explanations for how Ganesha came to have his elephant head. One of the most popular stories begins with the two great Hindu gods, Shiva and Parvati, who were husband and wife. One day while Shiva was away, Parvati created a son, Ganesha, by forming him out of mud. Parvati told her son to guard the door while she was bathing. But then Shiva unexpectedly returned home. Ganesha refused to let Shiva in. In a rage Shiva drew his sword and cut off Ganesha's head. Parvati ran to the doorway to see her son lying on the floor. She cried out. Shiva's heart broke when he realized what he had done. He vowed to replace Ganesha's head with the head of the first creature he found. The first living being that he encountered was an elephant. Shiva placed the elephant's head on the body of his son. Forever after Ganesha had the head of an elephant but the body of a human boy.

This Ganesha has four arms, which indicates that he is very powerful. In his hands he holds symbolic objects: two snakes, his own broken tusk, a large stick called an elephant goad, and a box of sweets, which he tastes with his trunk. His belly is round and his intricately carved ears are open wide to hear the prayers of his followers. Strings of beads drape his head, wrists, ankles, and neck, and he sits comfortably on a base with a pattern representing the petals of a lotus flower. This icon is quite small in size, so it was likely used in the home of an individual or family who might have rubbed the trunk or belly to bring good luck.

We do not know who the artist was because this statue is unsigned. It is carved from ivory, a valuable material that comes from the tusks of elephants. Because the Indian government has banned hunting elephants, artists today use bone for carving rather than ivory.

SHAHZIA SIKANDER. *The Scroll.* [Detail: for full panel see pages 2–3.]
1991–92. Vegetable color, dry pigment, watercolor, and tea on hand-prepared "wasli" paper. 16⅛" × 63⅞".
Courtesy of Sikkema Jenkins & Co.

Where is this scene taking place?

What story is this painting telling?

Can you find a person in this painting who appears more than once? How would you describe this figure?

Shahzia Sikander (b. 1969) grew up in a Muslim family in the city of Lahore, Pakistan. As a child she was interested in art, but it was not until she was a teenager that she decided to attend The National College of Arts in Lahore to study art seriously. While in school Sikander became determined to learn the techniques of miniature painting. She describes this as "an act of defiance," because at that time there was very little interest in this traditional art form.

India, Pakistan, and the surrounding regions have a rich history of miniature painting. Artists used tiny brushes to create images of people, animals, and places with intricate patterns and details, some of which can barely be seen without a magnifying glass. It can take many months or even years to create one small painting.

Miniature painters were hired by wealthy patrons to illustrate favorite stories, poems, or important events. Artists were not encouraged to express their own thoughts or feelings. Sikander transformed this approach, using the traditional techniques to create artworks that did express a personal or political point of view. In her work she often mixes styles from Muslim and Hindu traditions, ancient and contemporary images, and Eastern and Western symbols to create her own unique visual vocabulary.

In *The Scroll* Sikander departed from the small size of traditional miniature painting to create this long horizontal vision of a modern Pakistani house. The house walls and ceiling have been opened up so that the viewer can see into every room. In this detail from the painting, we see that the house is filled with people engaged in day-to-day activities such as relaxing, preparing a meal, cleaning, and playing. A ghostly young girl with long dark hair and transparent white clothing appears in several rooms of the house, unnoticed by the other adults and children. This figure represents Sikander herself as a young woman, observing scenes from her daily life in her home in Pakistan.

Crowned Buddha Shakyamuni.
Pala period, 11th century. India, Bihar. Schist. 27¾" high.
Asia Society, New York: Mr. and Mrs. John D. Rockefeller 3rd Collection, 1979.36.
Photo credit: Susumu Wakisaka, Idemitsu Museum of Arts, Tokyo.

What do you think you might know about the large center figure by looking at this sculpture?

What mood do you think he is in? How can you tell?

Why is one person big and other people are small?

Over 2,500 years ago, a young prince named Siddhartha Gautama was born the son of a wealthy ruler in what is now Nepal. His father was told that his son would grow up to be either a great king or a great religious teacher. Wanting his son to become a great king, Siddhartha's father kept him inside the palace, protected from the realities of life. When he was twenty-nine, Siddhartha slipped out of the palace and rode his chariot around it several times. Siddhartha witnessed people suffering, and this experience inspired him to seek the reason for suffering in the world.

For six years Siddhartha focused on meditating, praying, and fasting. One night, Siddhartha sat under a tree to meditate. During the night the evil demon Mara tried to distract him from his meditation. Siddhartha reached down with his right hand and touched the ground to call on Mother Earth to help him. When he touched the ground, he realized that people suffer when they become too attached to possessions. He reached enlightenment, a state of great wisdom and understanding. In this moment of enlightenment, Siddhartha conquered the demon Mara. He became known as the Buddha, which means "the enlightened one."

In this stone sculpture, the Buddha, the large figure in the center of the carving, sits calmly in the cross-legged or lotus position for his meditation. His left hand rests in his lap with the palm up, while his right hand reaches down to the ground. These hand gestures or *mudras* show us that this is the moment when Siddhartha touched his hand to the earth and reached enlightenment. The crown on his head and jewels around his neck symbolize his role as a universal supreme ruler, while the small dot on his forehead called an *urna* indicates his special wisdom. He is shown surrounded by four smaller versions of himself that refer to other important events in his life.

The Buddha spent the rest of his long life traveling and teaching in India. His followers are known as Buddhists, and Buddhism is one of the most practiced world religions today.

Katsushika Hokusai. *Village of Sekiya on the Sumida River,* from *Thirty-six Views of Mount Fuji.*
1832. Woodcut. 10" × 14^{15}⁄$_{16}$".
Photograph © Japan Ukiyo-e Museum.

What is happening in this painting?

How would you describe the setting?

If you were standing in this scene, what sounds might you hear?

Katsushika Hokusai (1760–1849) was born in the bustling Japanese city of Edo, known today as Tokyo. When he was eighteen years old, he became a student of the great woodcut artist Shunsho. For ten years while he learned the master's style, he also experimented with his own style.

Woodblock printing had been practiced in Japan since the eighth century, but mostly to make books, such as religious texts. Hokusai and others discovered that they could create an image with multiple colors. Publishers encouraged artists and printers to use these techniques to make pictures that could be sold and collected. These prints were called *ukiyo-e*, which means "picture of the floating world," because they showed scenes of everyday life and popular culture. *Ukiyo-e* were affordable because many identical prints could be made once the blocks were carved.

In 1823 Hokusai began a series of prints called *Thirty-six Views of Mount Fuji*. Although most *ukiyo-e* prints showed pictures of people, Hokusai decided to create a series of pictures that would show the many different perspectives of the great mountain. Mount Fuji is considered sacred to the Japanese and part of their folklore and religion. Each print in the finished series shows Mount Fuji in a different way. In many of the pictures, Hokusai included people from the countryside, showing them in the natural landscape with the mountain. The series took Hokusai eight years to complete, and it is considered one of his masterpieces.

In *Village of Sekiya on the Sumida River*, we see three riders racing their horses. The riders' heads are bent down and their robes billow behind them. Their raised path takes them above the standing water of the rice fields as they race away from the small house in the lower right-hand corner. A red Mount Fuji stands majestically in the distance, framed by the leaves and branches of a lonely tree along the path.

Hokusai was in his seventies when he completed *Thirty-six Views of Mount Fuji* in 1835. His desire to improve his art never left him.

TAKASHI MURAKAMI. *Jellyfish Eyes–MAX* & *Shimon in the Strange Forest.*
2004. Acrylic on canvas mounted on board. 59" × 59".
Courtesy Blum & Poe, Los Angeles. © 2004 Takashi Murakami/Kaikai Kiki Co., Ltd. All Rights Reserved.

What is happening in this picture?

Who are these characters and what kind of place is this?

What repeated shapes do you see?

What does the style of this painting remind you of?

When Takashi Murakami (b. 1962) was a boy growing up in Tokyo, Japan, he was very interested in *manga* (comics) and *anime* (animated cartoons and films). *Manga*, which means "random pictures," first developed in Japan in the 18th century, and famous artists published books of *manga* drawings. In Japan *manga* and *anime* became extremely popular in the 1980s, even though they are considered part of the *otaku* ("geeky" or "nerdy") culture.

Murakami's first artistic ambition was to be a science fiction animator. However, when he was seventeen he began taking a course in *nihon-ga*, a style of painting based on ancient Japanese artistic conventions. Murakami studied *nihon-ga* for eleven years, but during that time he also maintained his passion for *manga* and *anime*.

Murakami uses the term "superflat" to describe his work. Superflat refers to the two-dimensional flat shapes and colors in his work. He also uses this term to explain his effort to try to flatten the difference between "high art" that you might see at a museum, and art in popular culture.

Murakami has a staff of many assistants who help him make his art. He uses a computer to develop his ideas, but his assistants do the actual painting or building of his pieces. Murakami says that being part of a large group of people working together helps him to be creative. Takashi Murakami has shown his work all over the world, and he is a celebrity in Japan.

In this painting, we see a boy, Max, with his little dog, Shimon, standing on top of a large round shape. All around them swirl brightly colored circular shapes, which are eyes, complete with eyelashes, irises, and pupils. The artist has put himself into his own painting as the character Max. A faithful assistant is represented by the dog Shimon. They look out in wonder into the strange forest of jellyfish eyes, in a superflat world.

Scene from *The Tale of Genji,* from the chapter "The Maiden."
1650–1700. Six-fold screen, color and gold on paper. 2004. 67" × 141".
City of Detroit Purchase. Photograph © 1987 The Detroit Institute of Arts.

What do you think this image might be painted on?

What are the people doing?

Are the buildings close to one another? How can you tell?

Painted sliding or folding screens, such as this work, were used to divide the living areas or rooms in a home into spaces for different activities, such as eating, drinking tea, entertaining guests, or sleeping. These folding screens are known as *byobu*, which means "protection from wind." Japanese artisans were originally inspired by Chinese folding screens. Over time, however, they developed styles and themes that were unique to Japan.

Screens are made of sections of crisscrossing strips of wood covered by large sheets of paper to form a flat panel. An even number of panels are attached with nearly invisible paper hinges. The fully extended panels create a broad surface for a large painting. Folding screens were often painted with scenes of landscapes in different seasons or with stories from literature.

This screen shows scenes from "The Maiden," a chapter in a famous Japanese novel, *The Tale of Genji*. The author, Murasaki Shikibu, was a young noblewoman in eleventh-century Japan. Still considered one of the greatest works in Japanese literature, the novel tells the life story of Hikaru Genji ("the shining Genji"). Genji was a handsome, gentle, poetic, and loving prince who was considered the model for the ideal man. For hundreds of years *The Tale of Genji* has inspired artists, poets, and writers.

The screen is read from top to bottom and right to left. On the right side we see the House of Spring that belongs to Princess Murasaki. In her house Genji sits on green mats surrounded by court ladies in beautiful flowing robes. Cherry and maple trees, irises, and bamboo represent the four seasons. On the left side of the screen is the House of Summer where another lady lives. Below her house we see a magnificent horse in a stable. Nearby, three court ladies are artfully arranging flowers.

Each scene in the story is separated by clouds made of very thin layers of gold called gold leaf. The use of gold leaf indicated the wealth and high class of the owner. As in many traditional Japanese paintings, the artist does not try to create a sense of depth. Instead the elements of the scenes form a flat design of bold colors and bright patterns.

KIM HONG-DO. *Washing Place* (from Genre Painting Album).
1745–1806. Chosôn (late 18th century). National Treasure No. 527.
National Museum of Korea.

How many people do you see in this painting?

Why are two of the women beating the clothing with sticks?

Why is the action taking place on the bank of a stream?

What is the man in the hat doing? How can you tell?

Kim Hong-do (1745–1806) was born into a middle-class family in Korea during the Chosôn period (1392–1910). Although he was not a member of the *yangban*, the upper class, he was such a talented artist that he was hired by the king to be court painter. Kim (also known by his pen name, Danwon) produced many paintings on a wide range of subjects. He was popular during his lifetime and is most famous today for his realistic genre paintings.

Genre paintings depict the lifestyles and customs of a certain time period. Before the Chosôn period the lives of the common people in Korea were not often portrayed in artworks, and many artists painted subjects inspired by painters from China. During the Chosôn period there was an increased interest in exploring native traditions and subjects. Genre painters began to show all aspects of Korean culture and society in their artworks, not just the world of the privileged elite class. Fishermen, farmers, and carpenters were depicted going about their daily activities. Collections of these paintings were sometimes grouped together in albums.

Washing Place is from an album of genre paintings by Kim Hong-do. Kim's playful sense of humor is expressed in the moment he chooses to portray. A group of women are washing clothes on the banks of a stream while a man hiding his face with a fan peeps out at them from behind a rock. Kim leaves it to the viewer to imagine what might happen if the women discover the man's presence. The simple background with few lines and colors focuses the eye on the activities of the people.

Other paintings in this genre album provide glimpses into the lives of people from many levels of Chosôn society. Kim Hong-do's genre painting album is considered a national treasure in Korea.

Maebyong Vase.
Koryo Dynasty (mid-12th century). Inlaid celadon glazed porcelain. 11" high, 5" diameter at base.
National Museum of Korea.

What do you think this object might be?

What images do you see on the surface?

How would you describe the colors in this piece?

During the Koryo period (AD 918–1392), there were frequent exchanges of ideas and trade between Korea and its neighbor to the west, China. While the process of creating celadon ceramics (objects made from clay) originated in China, Korean artisans adapted and refined the process, raising it to new levels of quality and beauty. The term "celadon" refers to the greenish-gray glaze on this type of pottery. To create an inlaid celadon vessel, a potter would first shape it out of white porcelain clay either by hand or on a pottery wheel. Once the clay had dried slightly, a needle or wooden tool was used to etch a design into the surface. The carved design was then filled with slip (watered down clay), usually in the colors white, black, or green. This technique is called *sanggamm*, which means "inlaid," and it is unique to Korea. The vessel is fired in a wood-burning kiln, then glazed and fired again at a higher temperature. The celadon glaze provides the distinctive color but is translucent enough for the design to show through.

This particular vessel is a *maebyong* vase. The name refers to its shape: tall with a small mouth (opening), a short neck, rounded shoulders, and a slightly flared base. Some *maebyong* vases have been found that have a cup-shaped cover over the mouth, indicating that they may have been used to store liquids. The shapes of Koryo ceramics were inspired by forms found in nature. The simple elegance of this vase's gently curving S shape is an excellent example of the understated beauty valued and achieved by Koryo potters. Ceramic pieces of this time period were often unsigned, so we do not know the name of the artist who created this piece.

This vase is decorated with a design of graceful cranes and bamboo. The crane, a long-necked bird, is often used in Asian art to represent longevity (long life) and pure spirit. Bamboo is a plant that bends but does not break, even in strong winds and snow. It is seen as a symbol of strength and of the scholar, who does not change his views even under pressure.

◆

Go back and look through these pages again.

Which one of the artworks in this book stands out most in your mind today? Why?

What questions would you ask the artist about this work if she or he were here?

What things in these images seem familiar to you? What things seem new?

If you could visit one of the places that you read about in this book, where would you go?

Return to this book another day and you may see things in a different way. You may also discover something new about these Asian artists.

Keep looking!